Pearl Nsiah-Kumi

Your Maker Is Your Husband

PEARL NSIAH-KUMI

Pearly Gates Publishing, LLC, Houston, Texas

Your Maker Is Your Husband

Your Maker is Your Husband

Copyright © 2017
Pearl Nsiah-Kumi

All Rights Reserved.
No portion of this publication may be reproduced, stored in any electronic system, or transmitted in any form or by any means (electronic, mechanical, photocopy, recording, or otherwise) without written permission from the publisher. Brief quotations may be used in literary reviews.

Scripture references marked NIV and NLT are used with permission from Zondervan via Biblegateway.com

ISBN 13: 978-1-945117-96-1
Library of Congress Control Number: 2017960472

For information and bulk ordering, contact:
Pearly Gates Publishing, LLC
Angela Edwards, CEO
P.O. Box 62287
Houston, TX 77205
BestSeller@PearlyGatesPublishing.com

DEDICATION

This little book is dedicated to my friend and prayer partner of many years:

Jenny Prince!

God used her in so many ways to advise and encourage me during those difficult times. She encouraged me verbally and also through the many ways in which she supported me. I spent many nights in her home and, when necessary, she drove me to places I needed to be. It's wonderful to have a sister I also call a "friend".

Thank you, Jenny.

God bless you!

ACKNOWLEDGMENT

I thank **Pastor Wayne D. Lawton** for editing this book. Uncle Wayne (as my children and I called him) was the pastor of the first church—Layhill Free Methodist Church in Silver Spring, Maryland—I attended when I arrived in the United States.

Thank you, Uncle Wayne!

TABLE OF CONTENTS

DEDICATION VI

ACKNOWLEDGMENT VII

INTRODUCTION IX

CATEGORIZING "SINGLE WOMEN" 1

SINGLE CHRISTIAN WOMEN 5

WHY DO YOU NEED GOD TO BE YOUR HUSBAND? 10

GOD AS YOUR HUSBAND 12

- ❖ AUTHORITY IN THE HOME 12
- ❖ BEING UNDER THE HEAD AND LEADERSHIP OF YOUR HUSBAND 12
- ❖ LOVE 13
- ❖ TRUST 14
- ❖ PROTECTION 16
- ❖ PROVISION 18
- ❖ COMPANIONSHIP 22
- ❖ COMFORTING 23
- ❖ AFFIRMATION AND ENCOURAGEMENT 26
- ❖ CORRECTING 28
- ❖ DECISION-MAKING 29
- ❖ CHILDREN 31

YOUR MAKER IS YOUR HUSBAND! 33

YOUR INVITATION 35

ABOUT THE AUTHOR 38

CONTACT PEARL NSIAH-KUMI 39

INTRODUCTION

Talking about a husband means we are speaking of marriage. What is *marriage*? Marriage is the legal union of a man and woman. God instituted the first marriage in the Garden of Eden when He brought Eve to Adam and declared they were man and wife. Prior to that, God declared, *"It was not good for the man to be alone. I will make a helper suitable for him"* (Genesis 2:18, NIV). So, He did! He meant for them to be separated by nothing but death.

In the Book of Malachi, God said, *"For I hate divorce"* (Malachi 2:16, NLT). Later, Jesus said, *"A man leaves his father and mother and is joined to his wife, and the two are united into one. Since they are no longer two but one, let no one split apart what God has joined together"* (Matthew 19:5-6, NLT).

God's intention right from the beginning, when He created Adam and Eve, was to demonstrate the relationship between Himself and the Church and for the Church to replenish the earth with people in His image. However, not every person ends up in a marital relationship. Many single women feel shame and loss for not being in a marital relationship. My goal is to bring comfort to single women by pointing them to God's provision for them.

Likening Jerusalem to a widow, a childless woman, disgraced and shamed, God promised: *"Your Creator will be your husband"* (Isaiah 54:5, NLT). Your Creator is the Lord of Heaven's Armies, your Redeemer, the Holy One of Israel, and the God of all the earth (see Isaiah 54:5). If He has promised to fulfill a husband-role in the lives of single women, it must mean that women need the covering or umbrella that a man is called to be for a woman.

Pearl Nsiah-Kumi

CATEGORIZING "SINGLE WOMEN"

Are you a woman old enough to be in a marital relationship but find yourself single? Are you single by choice or is it due to circumstances beyond your control? Either way, which of the following four categories best describes your situation?

❖ You've never been married:
 If you have never been married, would you say it's because you haven't met "Mister Right" or that you'd rather stay single? Do you desire to get married and be able to have children? God knows the reason you're not in a relationship and He is able to change that—based on His plans for your life. But until He does, remember He loves you all the same. He wants to meet

your every need and make you feel content with your status as a single woman.

- ❖ You are Widowed:

    As a widow, you've been married before but lost your spouse. Obviously, there were responsibilities that landed unexpectedly in your lap. Do you long to remarry to fill the void left by the loss of your husband OR would you rather not go that route again? Have you found comfort in God, discovering that He is an amazing provider? He knows what will be best for you going forward. He'll take care of you!

❖ You are Separated/Divorced

Are you separated or divorced from your husband? What led to the separation? What did God say about it? Were you married to an unbeliever who wanted to leave or married to a believer you couldn't work out your differences with? I have been there, and although the reasons for our divorce or separation might be different, I can feel your pain.

Being a Christian woman, divorce never crossed my mind as a possibility. When I got married, I believed and pledged, "For better or for worse, until death do us part". I'll share a bit more about me later.

May God comfort you and give you the strength to carry on. He loves you!

- ❖ Lonely in a marital relationship that's going nowhere:

    Do you feel alone and lonely even though you are married? Don't despair; seek counseling with your pastor or a Christian counselor. Prayerfully seek wisdom and grace to be a godly wife for your husband, although you may feel like he doesn't deserve it. Until things turn around, God Himself will take on the husband-role and meet your emotional needs. God instituted marriage and knows what is missing in yours. Hang on to Him.

SINGLE CHRISTIAN WOMEN

I am speaking to the issue of being a single Christian woman because I'm in that place myself: God is **MY** husband!

I was married for almost 40 years and, together with my husband, we raised three children and now have four grandchildren. Yes, my husband protected us and was the lead in most of the decision-making. He cut the grass, washed the car, filled the gas tank, and did most of the taxiing around town as needed. So, you can imagine that when I left home to be on my own, I assumed responsibilities that I didn't have before. I was faced with yard work—both grass-cutting in the Summer and snow removal in the Winter. They were chores I did not care for, but they came with the territory of being single. I found them difficult and challenging, but I resolved those issues by hiring help. Now, my loving son-in-law cuts the grass for me, and I'm thankful.

You might be wondering why I left home after so many years of marriage. The truth is this: The complications of mental illness created a very unsafe environment for me. I had hoped my move-out would be temporary, causing the situation to change and allowing me to move back home again. In fact, I did not unpack all of my boxes when I arrived at my new address; I hoped that missing me would make him seek help so that I could return home. However, days turned into weeks, weeks into months, and months into years. He did not seek the help I desperately desired for him.

So, I went a step further and filed for divorce. At the time of this writing, nothing has changed. Where was God in all of this? After all, **HE** instituted marriage and hates divorce.

Still, He was with me and directed me through the counsel of some God-fearing individuals. God confirmed the counsel I received by saying:

"Without wise leadership, a nation falls; there is safety in having many advisers"
(Proverbs 11:14, NLT);

and

"Plans go wrong for lack of advice; many advisers bring success" (Proverbs 15:22, NLT);

and

"Don't go to war without wise guidance; victory depends on having many advisers"
(Proverbs 24:6, NLT).

So, I'm living a single's life. If that's your life as well — regardless of the reason — then let me assure you that you're not alone. Yes, scripture says God hates divorce (see Malachi 2:16), but as my counselor reminded me, God also hates murder. I didn't have much of a choice. It was either stay married and get hurt or killed, or move out. I chose to live, have God write the next chapter of my life, and have the opportunity to continue to pray for my children and grandchildren *(which, by the way, is a wonderful privilege)*.

If your husband is an unbeliever and leaves, the Bible says to let him go (see 1 Corinthians 7:15).

Your singleness might not have been the result of divorce. Maybe you haven't found the right man — or maybe you had one but he's now deceased. It's also possible that none of those instances apply to you. You could still be married, but things aren't going well and you feel alone. That was me for a number of years before I finally left home.

No matter how your singleness came about, our needs are similar and unique. I believe God has the answers we're each looking for.

WHY DO YOU NEED GOD TO BE YOUR HUSBAND?

Although God said it wasn't good for man to be alone, marriage is not meant for everyone. The Apostle Paul gives reasons why being single is okay; it has benefits.

"An unmarried man can spend his time doing the Lord's work and thinking how to please Him. But a married man has to think about his earthly responsibilities and how to please his wife. His interest is divided. In the same way, a woman who is no longer married or has never been married can be devoted to the Lord…I want you to do whatever will help you serve the Lord best, with as few distractions as possible" (1 Corinthians 7:32-35, NLT).

Your singleness might be a part of God's plans for you, even if you've been married in the past. You would need to know His mind regarding your singleness. Maybe He wants you to focus on ministry, as Paul explained in the referenced passage. If God is calling you to a life of singleness, He'll also make sure your needs are met. If you seek His direction, He'll show you which ministry He wants you to pursue. The best way to see that ministry succeed will be to stay focused and obedient to Him. As you follow His lead, you will experience His faithfulness in marvelous ways. He shows interest in even the minute details of our lives.

Embracing God as our Husband will help us find joy and contentment in our status as single women. How should we relate to Him in the husband-role? As we'll see, some of the responsibilities overlap because He's being both God and Husband to each one of us.

GOD AS YOUR HUSBAND

❖ *Authority in the Home*

The Church is the Bride of Christ and Jesus Christ is the Head of the Church, just as man is the head of the woman. In order for the woman to accurately reflect the role of the Bride of Christ—the Church—she has to have a cover: a husband.

❖ *Being Under the Head and Leadership of Your Husband*

Scripture teaches Christian couples to *"Submit to one another out of reverence for Christ"* (Ephesians 5:21, NLT). For wives, this command is further explained as submitting to your husband in all things, as to the Lord (see Ephesians 5:22-24). But since the

Lord is your Husband, you have all the more reason to submit to His authority. While we can disagree with our husbands about their decisions, we can comfortably accept God's headship because He is all-knowing and makes no mistakes!

❖ *Love*

God instructed husbands to love their wives (see Ephesians 5:25). We'll lack nothing here because God **IS** love. His motives for loving us are unquestionable; He loves us because He IS love and cannot do otherwise. All we receive from Him comes out of His love for us. We may have no human husband, but our Maker is our Husband—and He satisfies!

God also instructs wives to obey their husbands (see Ephesians 5:22), and that's not difficult to understand. Even if we each had a human husband, we would still need to obey Him as God.

❖ *Trust*

In order to have a close relationship with people—especially one's spouse—there must be trust and respect. The scriptures give us numerous reasons why we should find God trustworthy and dependable, whether as God or as Husband. He doesn't have different attributes for different roles. He is who He is—ALL of the time.

For example, the Psalmist reminds us of God's unchanging nature by saying, *"The Lord's promises are pure, like silver refined in a furnace, purified seven times over. Therefore, Lord, we know you will protect the oppressed, preserving them forever from this lying generation"* (Psalms 12:6-7, NLT).

Can you think of one single reason not to trust God? Everything He promises is as good as done. The Apostle Paul wrote to the Corinthians, *"All God's promises have been fulfilled in Christ with a resounding 'Yes!' And through Christ, our 'Amen'* (which means 'Yes') *ascends to God for His glory"* (2 Corinthians 1:20, NLT). Hence, trusting God should not be an issue for any child of God. None of His promises from the beginning of time has ever failed, nor will any fail in the future.

It is possible to have issues with His timing sometimes because we are impatient creatures of **NOW**, just like little children. The solution to the "NOW" attitude is learning patience. He commands us to *"Be still, and know that I am God!"* (Psalm 46:10, NLT). God is not man that He should lie or change His mind; He always comes through at the right time! Trust Him!

❖ *Protection*

Being protected is an indication of being loved. It is our God-given instinct to protect who and what we love. Being single doesn't make us any less loved. God has already demonstrated His love for us by dying in our place; He's secured a place for us in Heaven! He cannot love us any more than He already does, no matter which role He's in.

The scriptures tell us that after God gave up His Son for us, there's nothing else that He wouldn't do for us (see Romans 8:32). His promise to us is, *"Don't be afraid, for I am with you. Don't be discouraged, for I am your God…For I hold you by your right hand – I, the Lord your God. And I say to you, 'Don't be afraid. I am here to help you'"* (Isaiah 41:10, 13, NLT). *"So, if God is for us* (which He is), *who can be against us?"* (Romans 8:31, NLT). The answer is: **"NOBODY!"**

Be encouraged: If His eyes are on the sparrow, for which He didn't die, then be sure He is watching over you, day and night. Let's commit our ways to Him and rest in His peace.

"Be still", He says, *"and know that I am God"* (Psalm 46:10).

❖ *Provision*

God is our provider, whether or not we have a human husband. I saw this firsthand when I decided to move out and was looking for housing.

A friend's rental property was vacant, but it was taking me a bit longer to make the move. I asked her to not wait on me, but to go ahead and rent it out when she found a ready renter. She tried to find someone, but the place remained vacant until I was ready. As far as I'm concerned, God reserved that place just for me. Like Abraham said to his son, Isaac: *"God will provide…"* (Genesis 22:8, NLT) — and He did!

How has God been meeting your needs?

Quite often, He sends us help for needs we don't even know we have and, therefore, haven't thought of asking for. For example, without my asking, my neighbor cleared my snow (a chore that I did not care for) with his blower. It was a blessing!

Other times, He sends help from unexpected places. For instance, I had a conversation with a lady I met at an event that day. During our conversation, I mentioned I was scheduled for shoulder surgery in a few days. She gave me her contact information and asked me to call her if I needed help after my discharge from the hospital. Since my family lived out of state, it was encouraging to be reminded of God's ongoing provision. God made sure I knew He had everything under control and would provide all the care I needed — and He did!

Friends changed their work schedules to drive me to doctors' appointments, physical therapy appointments, and anywhere else I needed to go. In addition, they brought me food and all that I needed to stay comfortable. One such item was a recliner to sleep in because getting in and out of a regular bed after shoulder surgery would be difficult. I hadn't even thought about that myself. Furthermore, the friend who brought me the recliner wasn't loaning me her own recliner (she didn't have one herself); she borrowed it from another friend! What a wonderful God! What a wonderful Husband! He made arrangements for all I needed. His love overwhelms me!

Two years later, I was diagnosed with lymphoma and went through radiation. Again, my children and friends rallied around me (God's Ambassadors). There were many doctors' office visits for checkups and treatment. The first day I met the breast surgeon, she asked me if my husband didn't want to come with me (although my daughter was with me). I explained my situation to her. It was a bit awkward, one might say.

My out-of-town daughter made so many trips—14 hours round trip—to be there with me at the appointments. God designated people to support and encourage me. I went through both situations without a human husband, but I came through wonderfully, and because the Lord is my Shepherd, I never lacked a thing.

❖ *Companionship*

Who doesn't need or want companionship? Many singles I know express this need. Even after you've been out with friends for hours, when you get back home and are behind closed doors by yourself with no one to talk to, it becomes a different story! If you don't stay busy, loneliness could easily get you down.

How should one handle loneliness? I suggest reminding yourself often that the Lord is with you and to talk to Him. Tell Him what you're thinking or feeling, be it joy, pain, frustration, or whatever other emotion that you embrace. God is interested in all of that! He talks back to you by laying some thought or Scripture verse on your heart, or by getting someone to call or send a piece of encouraging mail your way.

Recently, I was down a bit. Out of the blue, I received a piece of mail from friends I hadn't heard from in a long time. They wanted to know how I was doing, and it cheered me up to know people care. Perfect timing! God knows exactly what and when to provide. Isn't He amazing?

❖ *Comforting*

Everyone needs comfort every now and then. Life is full of surprises, twists and turns, pain, sadness, and discouragement, making it necessary for each person to have someone they could call on for comfort when the need arises. After God created Adam (the first man), He said, *"It is not good for the man to be alone. I will make a helper who is just right for him"* (Genesis 2:18, NLT). Although the text doesn't say exactly what was on His mind regarding this 'helper', I'm sure comfort was one of the primary reasons.

Married women often turn to their husbands for comfort as needed. What about single women who cannot call on a husband? Should we just endure pain, discouragement, and sadness alone? No! God is our Husband! He can comfort us better than a human husband because He knows and understands our hearts without us ever saying a word.

In Luke 4:18-21, Jesus claims HE's been sent to comfort the brokenhearted (and trust me: He does). He whispers His peace that calms us. He comforts us through His Word as we meditate on it. Other times, He sends people our way to say the exact words we need to hear. Paul confirmed that when he said, *"God is our merciful Father and the source of all comfort. He comforts us in all our troubles so that we can comfort others"* (2 Corinthians 1:3-4, NLT).

As helpless as we 'singles' might seem, the Lord never forgets us. Let's call on Him in all situations! The Psalmist reminds us this way: *"Lord, you know the hopes of the helpless. Surely you will hear their cries and comfort them"*

(Psalm 10:17, NLT). Also, in Isaiah, He comforts us this way: *"The mountains may move and the hills disappear, but even then, My faithful love for you will remain"* (Isaiah 45:10, NLT). Amen!

The Lord lovingly reminds us that He'll never forget us. He says it this way: *"Can a mother forget her nursing child? Can she feel no love for the child she has borne? But even if that were possible, I would not forget you! See, I have written your name on the palms of My hands"* (Isaiah 49:15-16, NLT).

❖ *Affirmation and Encouragement*

Words of encouragement and praise go a long way to affirm one's abilities and strengths, building up the recipient's self-worth. Both women and men need affirmation; maybe women moreso than men.

The virtuous woman described in Proverbs 31 is trustworthy, bringing her husband good and not harm. She's hard-working, elegant, and provides for her household. She's wise and respectable; her children bless her, and her ***husband praises*** her (see verse 28). So yes, women need to be affirmed from time to time by their husbands.

Does not having a husband make us any less-deserving of praise and affirmation? No! God affirms us in ways that build us up by putting family and friends around us to fill that role. They may say things like, "You look nice today" or "You're hard-working" or "That was a good dish". Yet, we also need to learn to be okay with not being recognized or commended all of the time.

Always ask yourself what God thinks, smile, and go one with your day. I did that in my college days; I was single then, and it worked just fine.

❖ *Correcting*

In every healthy relationship, couples will need to correct each other; however, **HOW** it's done can profoundly affect the health of the relationship.

Correction or rebuke should not be accompanied by anger, insults, and bad attitude in order to be acknowledged, effective, and appreciated. Correction delivered with love and respect will be more effective.

Out of love, the Lord will correct us (see Proverbs 3:12). If we are stubborn and unrepentant, He will discipline us. His discipline is not meant to put us down; it is to help us to be transformed into His image. He says to us, *"I correct and discipline everyone I love"* (Revelation 3:19, NLT).

❖ *Decision-Making*

In a healthy marriage, couples consult each other and pray when they need to make a decision. The scriptures instruct us to not lean on our own understanding, but to acknowledge the Lord in everything, and He'll direct our path (see Proverbs 3:5-6). We 'singles' have a double reason to heed this admonition, since we don't have human husbands to consult in matters of decision-making.

When we fail to consult the Lord, outcomes can be devastating. For example, Joshua and the Israelites were deceived by the Gibeonites—neighbors they should have destroyed per God's instructions to Joshua. The Gibeonites hid the fact that they were the Israelites' neighbors, in order to make a treaty with the Israelites that would spare them. This is what the scripture says concerning that incident: *"So, the Israelites examined their food, but did not consult the LORD. Then Joshua made a peace treaty with them and guaranteed their safety, and the leaders of the community ratified their agreement with a binding oath"* (Joshua 9:14-15, NLT).

Three days after they made the treaty, the Israelites learned the truth. Of course, by then it was too late; they were bound by the agreement. Had they consulted the Lord, they would have done differently but instead, they were obligated to allow the Gibeonites to live—contrary to God's instructions (see Joshua 9:20-21).

❖ *Children*

If there are children involved, things can be more complicated. All the same, God does not change; His promises are sure. He'll provide and grant you wisdom and resources to take care of the children. Children of divorced parents experience emotional pain and discomfort, sometimes blaming themselves for their parents' breakup.

They need a lot of comfort, support, and encouragement.

My children were grown and gone before I left home, but even as adults, I know it hasn't been that easy for them. When they come to town, it feels a bit awkward as they visit both mother and father in different places, because before the separation and divorce, when they came to town, they came home to both of us.

The unmarried or widows with young children could find themselves playing the role of both mom and dad. Teaching the children to lean on the Lord will go a long way towards helping the children have the right focus and adjust to the changes.

YOUR MAKER IS YOUR HUSBAND!

My single friend, don't ever forget God's love for you! Walk with Him and serve Him faithfully. He'll never leave you alone. Before you call, He will answer; and while you're speaking, He will hear (see Isaiah 65:24).

Don't forget His promise: *"Do not be afraid, for I have ransomed you. I have called you by name; you are mine. When you go through deep waters, I will be with you. When you go through the fire of oppression, you will not be burned up; the flames will not consume you. For I am the LORD your God, the Holy One of Israel, your Savior"* (Isaiah 43:1-3, NIV).

As you look to the Lord for wisdom and provision, listen to His leading and follow His directions. He will show you who to consult about different issues. He will go ahead of you to prepare the hearts of individuals He will want you to consult; He will make sure you find favor with them. These could be lawyers, accountants, employers, government officials, and the like. Don't be afraid; God will always be ahead of you preparing the way.

Psalm 23 helps us comprehend more fully God's role as our Husband: *"The Lord is my Shepherd; I have all that I need. He lets me rest in green meadows; He leads me beside peaceful streams. He renews my strength. He guides me along right paths, bringing honor to His name. Even when I walk through the darkest valley, I will not be afraid, for You are close beside me. Your rod and staff protect and comfort me. You prepare a feast for me in the presence of my enemies. You honor me by anointing my head with oil. My cup overflows with blessings. Surely, Your goodness and unfailing love will pursue me all the days of my life, and I will live in the house of the Lord forever"* (NLT). God is our Husband; we have nothing to fear!

Your Invitation

In order to find this information helpful, the reader needs to have a personal relationship with God because the promises I reference were made to God's children—Christians.

If you are not already a Christian, you might be wondering how to become one or if a relationship with God is even possible. I have an answer for that concern:

We are all sinners and God's enemies. God, being just and Holy, must punish sin. But because He loves us, He provided a way for us to escape that punishment. He sent His one and only Son, Jesus, to die in our place. Our responsibility is to admit we are sinners, repent, and ask for His forgiveness through the finished work of Jesus. When we take this step, God forgives us and indwells us through His Holy Spirit. He adopts us into His family, making us His children. That's when a personal relationship with Him is established (see Romans 3:23; 6:23).

The Bible also says, *"Since our friendship with God was restored by the death of His Son while we were still His enemies, we will certainly be saved through the life of His Son. So, now we can rejoice in our wonderful, new relationship with God because our Lord Jesus Christ has made us friends of God"* (Romans 5:10-11, NLT).

The relationship with God, like any other relationship, needs to be nurtured to blossom. We achieve that through Bible reading, Bible study, prayer, and fellowship with other believers. It is also important to obey the Bible and share your faith with others.

After you take this step, you're ready to claim all of God's promises to enrich your life, including the ones in this book!

Your Maker Is Your Husband

Pearl Nsiah-Kumi

ABOUT THE AUTHOR

Pearl Nsiah-Kumi is a retired Registered Nurse and Christian Author. Born in Ghana, West Africa, she has lived in Maryland for over 40 years. She's divorced and has three adult children, one son-in-law, and four amazing grandchildren.

In addition to writing, she is also a volunteer at a Crisis Pregnancy Clinic where she ministers to women in crisis.

CONTACT PEARL NSIAH-KUMI

On the Web:

www.pearlkumi.com

Via Email:

pearl@pearlkumi.com

Pearl Nsiah-Kumi

www.ingramcontent.com/pod-product-compliance
Lightning Source LLC
Chambersburg PA
CBHW071545080526
44588CB00011B/1808